# Project Management for Entrepreneur

# Project Management for Entrepreneur

The essential tool to monetize and fast track your business growth

Nersa W. Dorismond

Copyright © 2019 by Nersa W. Dorismond.

| Library of Congress Control Number: | 2019900180 |
|---|---|
| ISBN: Hardcover | 978-1-9845-7563-0 |
| Softcover | 978-1-9845-7562-3 |
| eBook | 978-1-9845-7621-7 |

All rights reserved. No part of this book may be reproduced or transmitted in any form or by any means, electronic or mechanical, including photocopying, recording, or by any information storage and retrieval system, without permission in writing from the copyright owner.

Any people depicted in stock imagery provided by Getty Images are models, and such images are being used for illustrative purposes only. Certain stock imagery © Getty Images.

Print information available on the last page.

Rev. date: 01/11/2019

To order additional copies of this book, contact:
Xlibris
1-888-795-4274
www.Xlibris.com
Orders@Xlibris.com
790110

# Contents

Preface .................................................................................... ix
Introduction ........................................................................ xiii

Chapter 1: You ....................................................................... 1
   Become an entrepreneur or be an entrepreneur ..................... 1
   Quality of a business manager ................................................ 2
   Leadership ............................................................................... 2
   Selfish and stubborn ............................................................... 3
   Sociable and generous: give generously ................................. 4
   Be a visionary .......................................................................... 5
   Focus, focus and focus ............................................................ 5
   Keep the Momentum .............................................................. 7
   Disconnection murders the business person ......................... 7
   Sport ...................................................................................... 10
   Culture .................................................................................. 10
   Training for a better life ....................................................... 10
   Time management ............................................................... 11
   You and your partners? ........................................................ 14
Chapter 2: Your Business – managing your projects ............... 18
   Your business ....................................................................... 18
   Traditional company ............................................................ 18
   Franchise .............................................................................. 19
   MLM ...................................................................................... 19
   Buy or take over an existing business .................................. 19
   Project Management Success Tools ..................................... 20
   Let's talk the same language: define to better understand ... 20
   The triangle of success ......................................................... 20

| | |
|---|---|
| What is a project? | 21 |
| Project versus process | 22 |
| What is project management? | 23 |
| Planning categories | 23 |
| Cyclical planning | 23 |
| Upward planning, Agile method | 23 |
| Other definitions | 25 |
| Chapter 3: Annexe: A practical example | 45 |
| You are ready to start your project | 45 |
| Business file | 47 |
| What is modeling? | 48 |
| Make me a drawing | 49 |
| How will you monitor and control your project? | 55 |
| Conclusion | 56 |

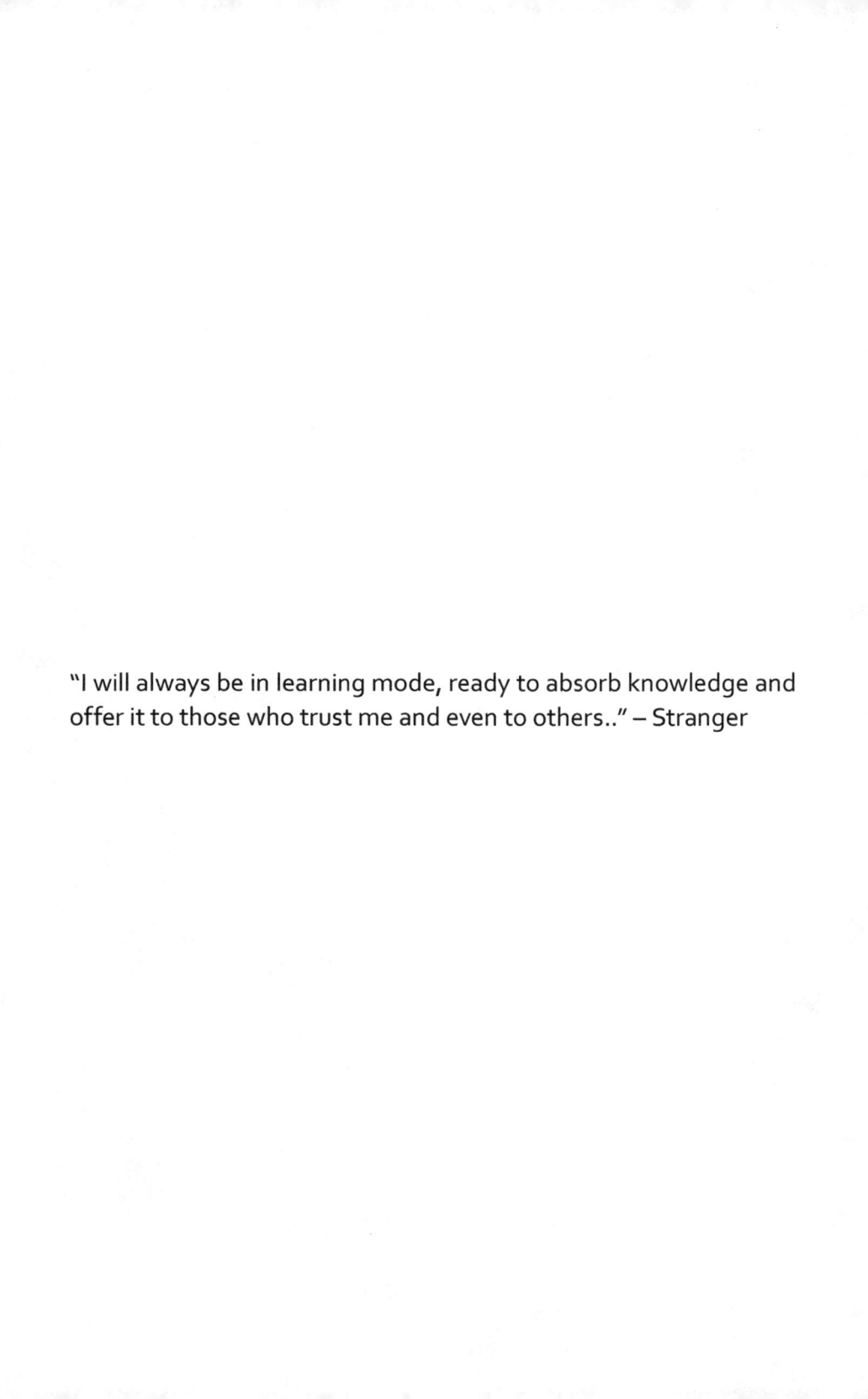

"I will always be in learning mode, ready to absorb knowledge and offer it to those who trust me and even to others.." – Stranger

# Preface

I wrote this book following several requests and questions from my students. I realized that institutional project management concepts were still relatively unknown at the *contractor* level and that the methodology was far from being leveraged to its full potential.

Considering this, I took it upon myself to reach out to the Montreal entrepreneur community in order to share my understanding of this science through practical examples that they can apply on a daily basis.

For more than 25 years, I have been working on corporate projects for others as well as for myself. Over time, I have acquired a deep knowledge of project management and we will go the most relevant practices and tools it in this simple and easy-to-read book.

What you presently hold in your hands is the accumulation of my academic, professional and entrepreneurial knowledge.

The result is a succinct but comprehensive definition of project management for entrepreneurs, something I had wanted to do for a long time and that I felt was definitely needed.

I have included a wealth of practical information that you can apply to your entrepreneurial reality.

Being an entrepreneurship myself for the past two decades, I can assure you that the information contained in this book is not merely theoretical but has been tested and retested in the field.

It is with pleasure and passion that I give you this little book on project management, so that you take the time to organize become more efficient and successful.

You can also follow me and discover new management tools on my website www.nersadorismond.com.

A work of this type and magnitude is never written alone hence I would like to take the time to thank the silent actors who pushed me into this adventure and kept me motivated throughout the years to complete it.

I would like to thank Vicky Rolfe in particular, who has put all her energy into dozens of revisions.

The collaboration between Ms. Rolfe and I is nothing new; we also worked together on my first book on the topic of the role of the project control officer (PCO).

Having started her own business in the past, Vicky soon realized a successful entrepreneur can benefit from understanding the basic principles of project management. Unfortunately, at the time, there were no book on this topic written specifically for entrepreneurs.

Ms Rolfe opted for the academic route and returned to school to complete a certificate in project management. When I approached her with the idea of writing a book on project management for entrepreneurs, she immediately accepted the challenge. Now that the English version of this book is finally available, I would like to take this opportunity to say that I am very proud to have worked with her on this project and that we look forward to publishing several more books in the future.

I would also thank Nathalie Dorsainville for taking the time to push me to finalize this book. Thank you to Richarson Dorvil for his support throughout the process and to Charles Brunelle for his help in the validation of project management techniques and his translation efforts.

"The Most Powerful Weapon for Changing the World Education." – Nelson Mandela

# Introduction

*a culture that rewards intelligent risk taking*

The world of entrepreneurship is not easy. At time it can be extremely difficult depending on your idea.

Multiply your initial estimate of the effort required by ten and you will have a good idea of the number of hours of work to complete to achieve YOUR dream of running YOUR business.

This incredibly rewarding and challenging experience will be worth every minute. It will force you to surpass yourself and overcome your fears.

Your friends and family will undoubtedly ask you: "why don't you choose this traditional path?" *metro-boulot-dodo* as we say in French.

**Turn your idea into a flourishing business...**
In the short run this decision may very well affect your diet and your sleep pattern. No one gets rich overnight but through it all of you must remember to believe in yourself and never give up.

A good way to start is to assess the market place, be on the lookout for new trends and find a product or service that provide a unique (and hopefully innovative!) customer value proposition.

**To get there you will need a plan...**
Evidently, you will also have to carry out a multitude of projects throughout the life-cycle of your business, and you will need learn how to **analyze, structure** and **implement** those ideas as well as **monitor** & **control** their results. I humbly offer this book to you, my second publication on this topic, it is a *concise* toolbox that hopefully contains all the information needed to succeed in

your projects and help you develop the fundamental technical background of a good entrepreneur

**Take into account all the little details...**
The book focuses on 3 aspects: **You**, Your **projects**, Your **environment**. We will cover all stages of project management: the planning phase, the project launch and the transition into operational mode and project closure.

"Start by conquering yourself even if you want to conquer the world." – Dr Victor Pauchet

# Chapter 1: You

You are the foundation of your company's success. You are the founder, the one who had the idea to found it. You are the visionary behind this idea that will allow you to achieve your freedom.

> The definition of freedom is unique to each person: some seek the freedom to work in accordance to their own schedule, while others aspire to attain wealth and money that their company will bring them.

You have the vision, ambition to succeed, and the personality to launch this first business project. You will need to write down your objectives and values, but most importantly, build a network of resources (a.k.a. stakeholders). This network will accompany you from the beginning of your adventure and will evolve over time.

**Become an entrepreneur or be an entrepreneur**
Some people were born with the mindset and need to start a business. They have this inner flame that will lead them to being heads of departments or come up with invention they made themselves. Those people have the entrepreneurial spirit: they build their first company at a very young age and have the flair that takes them to the top. We can say that they are project managers to the core. They will go through stages, keep their focus, build, and rebuild to always get closer towards the goal they have set for themselves.

Others become entrepreneurs by influence, destiny, or through learning. They often develop their entrepreneurial skills through training, seminars, or through their personal and professional experience. The Web is full of seminars, training, and books that can be very helpful for their personal development.

In either case, whether the entrepreneurial spirit is innate or acquired, the entrepreneur can succeed, provided that he is equipped with the right tools.

The entrepreneur will have to work tirelessly since the task will be difficult, requiring consistent perseverance, hard work, unfailing determination, and a compelling need to succeed.

The entrepreneur will also have to ensure that he has the necessary financial resources to support the evolution and development of his business until it is self-sufficient.

**Quality of a business manager**
A self-employed worker and a business owner are two distinct entities. Although, both are their own bosses, the business manager manages employees, while the self-employed worker only manages themselves.

To stand out as a business leader, you will need to work on the qualities that will help you succeed. Here is a list of these characteristics; they are based on my experience in the field. This list is neither complete nor exhaustive, but it is an excellent indicator of what you will need to acquire to carry out your business project.

- Sense of leadership
- Selfish and stubborn
- Sociable et generous
- Visionary
- Focus, focus, focus

**Leadership**
Leadership, a term borrowed from English, defines an individual's ability to lead or guide other individuals or organizations to achieve certain objectives. We will now say that a leader is someone who is able to guide, influence and inspire. A business leader must act

as a leader in order to influence his environment by infusing it with their own passion.

A project is born out of a brain-wave in your head. For you, this idea must become real. Although, clear in your head, this idea is only a vision and no one else but you understands where you are heading. It is therefore essential to convince those around you, and often complete strangers, to follow you in this adventure. Although, you pay some of your employees, it is important that they understand your vision, so that they remain motivated throughout their mandates. Being a leader in communication and sharing your vision with your team is fundamental.

The leader must adapt to their audience and the situation they manage. For example, in crisis situations, it is better to adopt a directive or even an authoritarian style. However, in times of growth, choosing a constructive style is the best of options to motivate your team. When you start your company, you need to have a unifying style in order to get people to work with you. If you do not have a leadership spirit, don't worry: there are many seminars and training courses to help you. You can also get help from a coach to help you, a mentor to guide you, or go back to school for a better education.

Foresight is better than hindsight: is a key rule the leader goes by. He must be able to adapt quickly to all situations by keeping his objectives and his team on the path of success. He is, undoubtedly, a mobilizer at all levels of the realization of his business projects.

**Selfish and stubborn**
Selfishness in entrepreneurship becomes a quality, a weapon of survival. Attention! I am referring to selfishness in the secrecy of your idea and not in the distribution of your product or service. The entrepreneur needs to be stubborn self-centered, a go-getter, and a dreamer. They believe in themselves and especially in their idea. They will therefore have to defend it fiercely to take it to where only

they, can visualize it. More importantly, they will have to protect it to avoid having it stolen.

As an entrepreneur, you will have to be a go-getter and an innovator. You will have to look for projects that will make you stand out so that you do not become those who have not succeeded. You are in control of your destiny and nothing must stop you. You are able to succeed if you put your mind into it, if you decide to succeed and if you dedicate your passion and time to your project. Don't let anyone tell you what to do. However, listen to advice and see how you can integrate it into your vision. Be the student of those who have succeeded before you. If you don't have the answers to your questions, then take the time to learn, be informed and innovate. However, always protect yourself: vultures will be on the lookout for what you are doing and will try to destroy it.

> Mind you, letting someone else steer my boat is a reality I've experienced. It turned out to be a very bad idea. By letting someone else start your business, tell you what to do, and how to do it, you will start to doubt your ability to run it successfully.
>
> Stay in control of your creation; your dream, while remaining informed and above all, open to improvement. I like to believe that all ideas are good. What makes the difference is how you will make them happen.

**Sociable and generous: give generously**
"Give and you shall receive" is a saying that is well known to all successful entrepreneurs. It is the law of attraction: by giving generously to others, you attract benefits of all kinds. It is important to understand that, in the business world, giving does not mean giving your idea. We are talking about offering customers something more, so that they can remember your product, or giving your employees more time and explanation, valuing their work, etc.

Give your customers a little something extra, so they will want to come back and buy an extra product or just talk about you.

## Be a visionary

An entrepreneur is a visionary, a madman in his art, who sees what the majority does not. Being a visionary means anticipating what will happen based on an idea, a dream. The entrepreneur has a clear idea and knows specifically where he sees himself in the future. Even if he does not have the financial resources, he is heading for the life he created in his mind. This practise is called transportability. It will attract the key elements for project achievement and success. Unfortunately, many are called, but few are chosen. To achieve this, the entrepreneur will have to be passionate about what they do, work tirelessly, and have a strong desire to achieve a goal they have set for themselves. A business leader must have a strong devotion to get there.

## Focus, focus and focus

To succeed in what you are about to do, you will have to focus on the objective you have set for yourself. Being focused means staying enthusiastic about the objective you have set for yourself, without scattering, or losing motivation. Maintaining this motivation, which is normally omnipresent at the beginning of the project, is the only way to achieve this. There are several ways to stay focused, and here are some important ones:

- Always know what others' expectations are and ask them what they want, so you can focus on them. You should do this by asking questions about the person's deep goals.
- Set firm deadlines for each task or activity you need to do, considering your priorities. When you complete the task on time, you will feel satisfied and get the job done.
- Plan your week according to priorities. Choose your appointments and evaluate the requests received to see if they fit your business strategy.

- Complete the projects you undertake and complete your achievements. Choose your projects, plan them, stay focused on what you are doing, and carry them out to the end.
- Fix the problems you encounter immediately: don't leave them lying around, because they will negatively affect your professional and personal life.

By maintaining emphasis on what you have to accomplish, you will allow yourself to prevail in your tasks.

Confining: Causes and outcomes of disappointment

There are a few reasons for disappointment in the life of a business visionary. Some are capricious and others can be controlled as utilizing the accompanying:

A correspondence, a gauge of the costs, the calendar or the assets, change administration, and the meaning of the edge.

Here are a few insights on the most well-known reasons for disappointment when arranging an undertaking.

- 40% Range changes
- 36% Availability of human or material assets
- 33% improbable conveyance time
- 28% Objectives not cleared up - what would you like to do?
- 19% because of poor correspondences
- 19% Wrong arranging prompts a task that won't succeed
- 18% Customers or clients are not locked in
- 16% Lack of administration
- 14% Lack of abilities inside the undertaking group
- 10% Poor gauge of expenses and timetable

## Keep the Momentum

When we are independently employed or pioneers of our organization, we should self-inspire constantly to continue pushing ahead. The main individual who can guarantee your prosperity or disappointment is yourself. You should get up each morning and make another stride in the acknowledgment of your business. There is nobody to give you your plan for the day, assess you, give your compensation like clockwork, or give you a pay increment. There is just you. How to keep Momentum? By chipping away at you and your characteristics:

- The enthusiasm of your undertaking which is an essential piece of your DNA.
- The dauntlessness to go ahead and clarify that what you will accomplish is the loveliest thing
- The imagination to re-examine yourself and take individuals on your way
- Acceptance of disappointments and the quality to stand up and continue pushing ahead
- The focal point of moving with extra special care towards the last objective

## Disconnection murders the business person

The lion's share of new companies confront confinement. Being distant from everyone else and overseeing everything in the organization (publicizing, deals, advancement, bookkeeping, administration, bundling, organizing, and so forth.) frequently prompts dejection. Notwithstanding this forlornness, he, as a rule, does not have sufficient energy to center around building up his private company into a medium or extensive organization.

There are diverse approaches to arrive:

- Create a motivation in which you plan time for games, to meet different business visionaries, to take training and to

make yourself known somewhere else than by means of web-based life.
- Take, prepare, and arrange
- Go find help at an affordable cost

1. A few gatherings have grown free occasions to enable you become well known: Facebook, LinkedIn, and Eventbrite are great suppliers of occasions.
2. Enterprise focuses can likewise enable you to more readily structure your business and your pioneering life. Each and every tip will influence you to develop.

Go to meetings, online classes, and workshops where you can find out about your advancement and that of your organization. Proceed to pass your cards, as well as to gain from others. You could create fascinating associations and additionally go searching for new clients and markets. Examining between business people makes it conceivable to discover answers for your issues and not to feel alone in your reality. I don't detract from web-based life the way that they have made it conceivable to not generally need to head out to meet clients or create. Be that as it may, it regards setting aside the opportunity to shake hands with other people who are in circumstances indistinguishable from yours and talk about your existence.

**Social Media** will allow you to expand your customer base as well as build relationships with your employees and partners outside of corporate communication channels. Traditionally, creative industries were early adopters of social media *in lieu of* corporate press releases, but as a recent forbes.com article (*) points out, this concept of social media personality is spreading across the spectrum of consumer goods.

Source: https://www.forbes.com/sites/forbesagencycouncil/2018/06/03/if-you-want-to-humanize-your-brand-on-social-media-try-these-10-tactics/#2dd38744d2e0

**Networking** is an inexhaustible source of new customers and luckily for you, there is no shortage of trade fairs, conferences, professional associations and sporting events. Do not hesitate to take time out of your busy schedule. Evidently, it may take a lot of energy to travel back and forth to a major city, but view it as an opportunity to grow your network and win new contracts down the line. In the short term, you will also be exposed to new perspectives and will gradually improve your communications skills. You would be amazed at the number of entrepreneurs with whom you could develop a long-term business relationship and even partnerships.

Customer relationship Management (**CRM**) tools *use data analysis about customers' history with a company to improve business relationships with customers, specifically focusing on customer retention and ultimately driving sales growth* (source: Wikipedia). I would also add that sending the right message at the right time and with the proper communication channel will help you increase your NPS (see below), especially as a young relatively unknown company. *Net Promoter or Net Promoter Score (NPS) is a management tool that can be used to gauge the loyalty of a firm's customer relationships. It serves as an alternative to traditional customer satisfaction research and claims to be correlated with revenue growth. NPS has been widely adopted with more than two thirds of Fortune 1000 companies using the metric. The tool aims to measure the loyalty that exists between a provider and a consumer. The provider can be a company, employer, or any other entity. The provider is the entity that is asking the questions on the NPS survey. The consumer is the customer, employee, or respondent to an NPS survey. An NPS can be as low as –100 (every respondent is a "detractor") or as high as +100 (every respondent is a "promoter"). A positive NPS (i.e., one that is higher than zero) is generally deemed good, and an NPS of +50 is generally deemed excellent.* Your personal life: a necessity. The number one rule in business is not to mix personal and professional life. Always working from home gives the impression of always having to work. It is important to remember that you must set time for your family, friends and significant other. It is important to take care of your business, to reduce your business costs, and take a step back from your business. This decline will encourage an open mind on your work and your creativity. Plan this time in your calendar as an appointment with yourself.

### Sport
Practicing sport can be a good alternative to loneliness, because many disciplines are practiced in groups. Why not organize running, cycling, or any other sports sessions with your employees? It is well known that the best contracts were signed on golf courses. This is an opportunity to socialize with your employees and stay healthy. You can also join existing Volleyball or Badminton groups, for example.

### Culture
The cure for loneliness
As an entrepreneur, it is crucial to take time for yourself: go to concerts, visit a museum or simply discover new landscapes. Whether through reading, sports, music or cinema, let your mind escape somewhere else. Don't feel guilty when you take time for yourself, because letting go will help you to perform better.

### Training for a better life
There are different ways to acquire the knowledge you need to succeed. You need to be trained while keeping an open mind to absorb as much information as possible. There are various types of training to acquire the skills you need to fulfill your potential and develop your business, such as:

- Audio books
- In-class courses (at entrepreneurship centers for instance)
- E-learning (online)

**My definition:** Vocational training is a process that allows an individual to learn and acquire knowledge or know-how, i.e. the skills and competencies necessary for an occupation. Training can also provide professional expertise in a specific field that the company or simply the individual wants to acquire.

The training allows participants to be more efficient and dynamic within the company. It is an essential tool to stand out from your competitors. Even if you are the only one starting your business, you need to take the time to acquire the knowledge to grow it. The web is full of free training courses, audio or virtual books that can provide you with the information you need to develop your effective entrepreneurship. Amazon, Udemy, YouTube, or your local library are full of free information.

**Time management**
Time is not extendable. There are only 24 hours in a day and sleep is a necessity that takes at least 6 hours. Of these remaining 18 hours, we must consider time losses such as traffic, subway breakdowns and so on. A question arises: how to manage your time effectively? There are different planning techniques to know and you need to pick the one that is right for you.

Personally, I apply the same method on my schedule: if I have an appointment at rush hour, I give myself a larger time margin than if I have an appointment at a regular time during the day. I also use the color method to determine the order of importance and categorize my appointments. Finally, I write my reports and cancellations with a pencil in my paper agenda. This allows me to make corrections if necessary.

There are also several books on time management. I advise you to read: Efficiently *Manage Your Time and Priorities*, by Daniel Latrobe. He explained that time management can be summarized in 3 components:

Time management is:

- perform a set of **tasks**
- under **time constraints**
- to achieve a **goal**

Often, we try, through different ways to optimize our time and complete ALL our tasks. Is this realistic? I don't think so. It is impossible to perform all tasks at the same time. It is therefore essential to talk about prioritization.

**Definition of prioritization: Prioritization is assessing elements to determine which one should be executed before the other, according to an order you have established. Ex: You have an appointment with a service provider for the development of a partnership. A customer asks you for an appointment at the same time to provide information about your services. Which of the two appointments can be moved? It depends on the task that is most important to you at that very moment.**

*Prioritization Technique:*
Before prioritizing, you need to know what you have to do. Make a list of your tasks and give them a value (1 important, 2 less important, 3 not important). You also need to learn to turn down additional last-minute tasks or appointments. By making a daily list, it is easier to see what is urgent, what can be postponed, and even what can be cancelled.

Here are some techniques that will help you classify your tasks (if you do some basic research you will find more techniques, I only propose those two):

1. Trash, washing-machine, treasure

    ◦ In the trash: all the ideas that you consider less relevant and will take a long time without giving you immediate added value.

- In the washing machine: all the ideas you need to keep, but are not necessary or usable in the present moment. Leave them there for future analysis.
- In the treasure: the ideas you need to plan, because they are the most important in the present moment.

As you can see, this technique uses an analogy to help you define the order of importance of your tasks.

2. MoSCoW

   There is another technique called MoSCoW. It is a nuanced technique which looks like the one mentioned previously:

   - **M**: must have this, (vital).
   - **S**: should have this if at all possible, (essential).
   - **C**: could have this if it does not affect anything else, (comfort).
   - **W**: won't have it this time but would like in the future, (luxury, budget-related optimization).

3. The Eisenhower Matrix

   The Eisenhower Matrix, on the other hand, uses two axes to validate the importance of the action or task to be performed.

|  | URGENT | NOT URGENT |
|---|---|---|
| IMPORTANT | DO<br>Do it now | DECIDE<br>Schedule a time to do it |
| NOT IMPORTANT | DELEGATE<br>Who can do it for you? | DELETE<br>Eliminate it. |

These techniques can provide you with the time you need to develop your project by reducing the number of non-priority tasks.

It is necessary to analyze your priorities regularly to keep control. Add this activity to your agenda on Sundays, for example, before starting a new week.

**You and your partners?**
Several entrepreneurs have tried to team up with a partner to better develop and operate their business. According to the Civil Code:

> "Art. 2186. A partnership contract is one by which the parties agree, in a spirit of collaboration, to carry on an activity, including running a business, to contribute to it by pooling goods, knowledge or activities and to share the resulting benefits among themselves."

This means that the partners must work as much as each other and accept the company's ups and downs. Risks must also be shared.

People often try to start a business with one or more partners by thinking that there is strength in numbers. Some unions have indeed been successful: think of Bill Gates and Paul Allen, the founders of Microsoft for example. Others quickly went sour: the AOL-Time Warner merger is undoubtedly one of the most memorable. Always keep in mind that a business association implies that the partners share the same vision and, above all, understand that the primary goal is the development of the company and not the individual.

How to choose a good business partner? The key to success is simple: you must proceed as if you were looking for an employee! Look at your potential partner's CV, ask about his or her values and professional beliefs and make sure they are a good match with yours. Complete a questionnaire as if you were being interviewed and review your answers together. I often suggest that entrepreneurs wishing to join forces should grant each other a probationary period, i.e. a period during which both parties can put their partnership to the test. You can also ask a third party to validate the feasibility of your association.

Do not accept the first one who comes a long, simply because you know them or because they promise you the world. Take the time to observe and get to know the individual before you connect. At the slightest doubt, abstain, because instinct is strong. Your inner voice may be signaling to you that he is not your ideal partner.

Once your partner has been validated, all you have to do is write the terms of your agreement using a contract. The contract must clearly indicate the rights and duties of each party. Don't wait too long before putting them on paper. The contract should be drafted at the beginning of your alliance, when everything is going well and you are on good terms. As with any alliance, the strength of a "resolute" contract will prevent your project and business from falling apart. Contact a business law specialist who will draft your contract and discuss the limits and rights of each party.

Signing an "NDA" (non-disclosure agreement) is a wise strategy to protect you and your future partner. This agreement is intended to prevent your idea from being copied or stolen.

An associate and a partner are two distinct parts. Do not mix the two and must choose the one that is most interesting for you. A partner is either a person, a company or an entity that invests its knowledge, money or both in your business. A partner is a professional or a company that offers to meet a particular need to help you. The partner has no interest in the company's capital in the short term.

Having a business partner may also mean that you are giving up a percentage of your business. Do not give your shares without careful reflection, because you could lose the right to your company and even your company in the mid or long term. Take your time and carefully validate the reasons why this partnership is necessary. Always keep in mind that this is your project. If the idea is common then work on an agreement that will be mutually beneficial.

If you choose to fly on your own but need a helping hand, hire a contractor instead of a partner. This person will therefore not have a share in your company.

"Take the first step in faith. You don't have to see the whole staircase, just take the first step." – Martin Luther King Jr.

# Chapter 2: Your Business – managing your projects

**Your business**

Some entrepreneurs are fortunate enough to know exactly which industry they want to start in and will work in that direction. For others, it's the passion of being their own boss that makes them want to own a business.

The vision of being an entrepreneur is attractive. On the other hand, many will stop at the fact that they have no idea of what type of business they would like to start or are not convinced that the idea they have in mind can work. It is, therefore, important to know that there are several alternatives to the traditional business. These alternatives are generally divided into four types of companies, but all fall into these categories:

- Traditional business: you create your own system
- Franchise: you buy an existing system - may turn out expensive
- MLM (Multilevel Sales) or Personal Franchise: You become a member of an existing system - minimum cost and often monthly.
- Buy an existing business or take over an existing business

**Traditional company**

The traditional enterprise is the type of joint venture of the future among the future entrepreneurs. It consists of creating a need (product or service) and turning it into a system that will generate profits. This type of business has a very high-risk factor due to the time and energy costs that flow from it. Indeed, many people go into debt to get there and do not always succeed in realizing what they planned.

### Franchise
Some people go into business by buying a franchise from an already established company whose system is already running and has proven itself. Buying a franchise is about managing a brand for someone else. Just like a traditional business, you need to look for a good location, premises, manage staff, manage inventory, and manage the competition. We must also pay a discount to the mother house. Very few people can buy a franchise because the cost is extremely high.

### MLM
Since the beginning of the century, a new type of business has taken shape: the MLM. MLMs create a business under an existing banner (mini-franchise) without the investment, risk, expense, personnel, inventory, equipment, administration, and professional knowledge that other types of business require. Many people around the world owe their success to MLMs. Nowadays, the greatest economists and businessman have set it up as the "21$^{st}$ century enterprise".

### Buy or take over an existing business
Buying or taking over an existing business is an alternative interesting. However, we must analyze it, weigh the pros and cons, and validate if this option is the best for you. The advantage of this type of business is that, normally, the previous owners have done all the startup work and the business is already running. This option can be expensive. It is therefore advisable to seek the help of a specialist to assist you in your efforts.

## Project Management Success Tools

In this chapter, we will talk about the science of project management. Although complex, I have selected here the most useful concepts to meet your specific entrepreneur needs. This schematic adaptation of project management will allow you to increase your level of performance and succeed in the different projects that you will achieve for your company. It will also allow you to understand the actions you should take and especially how to properly monitor and control your business.

The first project you are going to set up is launching your business. Before you embark on this new adventure, it will be necessary to validate your idea. This means you will need to do the market analysis and see if your idea meets a need. In the next chapter, we will review a case study to help you launch your business

> Note: in this chapter when we say project manager, we refer to you as the person who will realise the idea. But you also can give it to a specialist.

## Let's talk the same language: define to better understand

Here are some important definitions that put into context the notions that we will see in the next pages.

## The triangle of success

The whole structure of this modern methodology of project management is based on the concept of the triangle of success. This symbol, widely used, was popularized by Harold Kerzner who speaks in detail in his book "Project Management: A Systems Approach Planning, Scheduling, and Controlling." This project triangle demonstrates the relationship between time, cost ($) and goal (range) elements. The adjustment of one of these three factors has impacts on the other two.

The three axes represent the fundamental points of the making of a project. Changing one of these axes can easily confuse the current project. It will be the project manager who will aim to prevent the complete disintegration of the triangle by ensuring to continually rebalance the axes of the triangle to reach the project delivery goal.

**Distinction between objective (why) and content (what)**

| | |
|---|---|
| Budget | The cost of the project is the sum of the expenses of the human and material resources and / or software of the project. The cost depends on the duration of the project |
| Scope | The scope of the project is a general description of the features and functions that qualify the product, service, or outcome that the project seeks to deliver or achieve |
| Time | Deadline: change or modification of the planned dates that impact the final date of the project. Scheduled date at which an activity or a global project begins and ends |

**What is a project?**
The PMI® defines the project as "a temporary enterprise, initiated to provide a product. "A project" is a finalized set of activities and actions undertaken with the aim (scope) of meeting a defined need within set deadlines and within the limit of a budget (cost) allocated.

A project is a set of activities that take place according to a deadline, producing a certain type of result. Some projects are self-sustaining, that is, they are not related to any work done within an organization. Others, on the other hand, fit into a broader framework of phases, processes, programs, and portfolios.

**Project versus process**
The process in "project mode" differs from the process in "operational mode". An activity conducted in a project mode is generally not intended to be repeated, which leads to some uncertainty about its control. An operational project, on the other hand, is intended to last and generally does not have a planned end date.

Our modern societies have become "project-mode societies"

"The projects concern as much of the institutions (school project, hospital project, bill, political project, social project, etc.) as the individuals (holiday project, retirement project, professional projects, family, business, etc.).

This presence of the project mode in all aspects of our life refers to an idealized vision of this mode of action. This utopia then seems to have become an instrument giving hope to man to no longer grieve the events. It now allows him to master the course of history and forge the future in his own way. What are we talking about exactly? What is really hiding behind this magic word supposed to be a miracle cure for men and organizations of this turn of the century?

The main advantage of the process in "project mode" is the holding of deadlines in the design and delivery of project elements. This mode allows better control of budgets and execution.

As a business owner, you need to be aware of how much money you will spend throughout the life of your business. You need to make sure that every dollar is spent in the right way by validating the return on your investment (ROI). We will come back to this concept shortly.

## What is project management?

According to Wikipedia, "it's a process of organizing, end-to-end, the smooth running of a project. It is all the operations and tactics that makes a project succeed in a triangle representing the quality-cost-delay (QCD). The management of the project in the difference assumes the strategic management of the project."

According to the PMI® "it is the art of directing and coordinating human and material resources throughout the life cycle of a project using appropriate management techniques to achieve predetermined objectives: costs, deadlines, quality, customer satisfaction, and participant satisfaction."

When project management involves the delivery of a set of related projects, these are part of what we call a "program". When a set of projects within a company are not interrelated, we are talking about 'portfolio management'.

## Planning categories

### Cyclical planning

Cyclical planning often adopts the name of "classical method". This is characterized by a predictive approach of "cascade cycle" that involves the forecasting of sequential phases. Make sure to validate the previous step before moving on to the next one. The project manager must then engage in a planning precise: collect the needs, define the product, develop it, and test it before delivering it. He will also have to carry out the project by foreseeing validation steps called milestones of the beginning and end of the phase. These milestones will help him to control the project.

### Upward planning, Agile method

Upward planning favors simpler project designs, shorter project cycles, effective collaboration between team members, and better customer engagement with team members. It also uses a more structured decision-making system. This trend is generally known as "agile project management".

It is suggested to use a combination of the two techniques presented above, accompanied by small launches during the project, to eliminate certain risks and obtain results quickly.

## Other definitions
***Operations:*** Operations are the activities and common tasks that are necessary for the proper functioning of your business. Unlike the project, they have no beginning or end. Example of operation in a company:

***Project:*** Launch of a client management tool. Purpose of the project: put in place of a CRM with the resulting processes.

***Operation***: The use of the tool by the different members of the organization.

***Company:*** According to Wikipedia, a company is "an economic unit, legally autonomous and organized to produce goods or services for the market". In a company, these are constant efforts that bring about recurring results.

You must clearly distinguish between a project and operations: a project is the realization of a need. Operations are the activities that follow the implementation of a project. Example: You want to create a timesheet tool to collect the hours of your employees. This project has a purpose, a beginning and an end. When the timesheet is implemented, the project will be completed. This time sheet will become a tool in the operations, helping your employees to record their time.

## Project actors and your company's stakeholders
When you start a business alone, you are considered self-employed. As soon as you have employees, you become a business leader. In both cases, you oversee several departments since you are the supreme leader. You must take care of accounting, marketing, finding customers and producing your product or service.

## Project actors

As explained earlier, a project is a temporary structure. When you want to bring a project to term, you must put together a team of people who will help you to achieve it. These people are called project actors. This team of actors is ephemeral and will be in place only during the life of your project.

It is very difficult to set up a business without being surrounded by one or more resource people: accountant, computer graphics, Webmaster, and other resources. These resources are essential to the smooth running of your project. They can be part of the business or just around you.

## Stakeholder

A stakeholder is a legal or physical person who can be positively or negatively impacted by the project. A stakeholder has an interest in promoting themselves in the project, whether in terms of signing a contract, a sale, an employee, an outside expert, or a supplier. It is therefore essential to communicate with them.

- Identify stakeholders
- Plan the management of stakeholders
- Manage stakeholders
- Control the management of stakeholders

## Project management versus project management

Throughout the life of your business, you will have to set up initiatives: from the smallest idea, to the realization of big projects. Whether it's launching your business, installing a new software, setting up a CRM, a hiring process, an email system, etc., all this will have start and end dates. These initiatives represent a series of unrelated projects within the same company, that is, a portfolio of projects. Your role as a business leader is to manage this portfolio. Each project must be analyzed, approved, planned, and finally closed. Once you master these steps, you will be in control and will be able to choose the right project that follows your business strategy and that will not waste time and money.

**Planning and top-down analysis, portfolio management**

It concerns the portfolio of projects (list of needs for development for the organization of the company) that an organization must have as well as the possibility of making portfolio information more transparent, thanks to data mining technologies. We are talking here about choosing and carrying out the right project at the right time.

In addition, project management is equipped with cost measurement tools and a set of monitoring and control tools that apply to all stages of a project. Thus, each decision maker can know at any time what a project costs and what financial resources are already committed. This specific characteristic of the organization in "project mode" then makes it possible to apply management policies related to "project management" (ex: forward planning, risk measurement, corrective action plan, etc.).

**Life cycle of a project**

| Phase | Description | Définition | Document to be produced |
|---|---|---|---|
| *Pre-launch* | *Define the benefits of setting up this new project* | *Validate the feasibility of the idea with a business case* | *Business file* |

| | | | |
|---|---|---|---|
| **Start (project launch)** | *Define the outline of the project to be realized and obtain the necessary authorizations* | *Validate if our idea can be realized. Prepare the outline and get permission to continue the project.* | *Project Charter* |
| **Project planning** | *Provide all the necessary tools for its perfect realization.* | *Structure what we will do.* | *Project plan Risk Management Plan Project schedule Organization chart of projects (WBS))* |
| **Development (Project execution)** | *Start the project, monitor its evolution and control every detail.* | *Put in place what was planned for the realization of the project* | |
| **Closing (Closing the project)** | *Close the project after all plans have been respected* | *Ensure that the set up at the operations is done adequately* | *After death* |

| | | | |
|---|---|---|---|
| **Monitoring and control** | *Ensure customer satisfaction* | *Throughout the project monitoring indicators will be put in place to validate its control* | *Dashboard*<br><br>*Action registry*<br><br>*Progress Report* |

It is important to follow certain steps to achieve your project. At each of these stages, a checkpoint will be set up to confirm that you can proceed to the next step. The life cycle of a project refers to all the steps that allow a project to evolve from a basic idea to its final realization. There are two methods of project realization by step: the cyclic and incremental method.

The cyclic method allows you to take an idea to its realization by going through 5 steps. The start-up phase (the idea) until its transfer to operations following the closing phase. This cycle is divided as follows:

**Pre-start phase: project opportunity**
Pre-startup is to see if the idea you want to achieve comes from a need or an opportunity, if it fits into the company's strategy, and if you have the means to set it up. Here, you will prepare what is called a business case. It sounds complex but, on the contrary, it is only a small document that will help you make the right decision.

The exercise will save you money and time and make sure it's really what you need. It will also allow you to make the right choice of project.

Once this document is completed, take the time to choose the project with a high ROI - the portfolio management that I presented before will help you do that.

| Sujet | Description |
| --- | --- |
| **State of the current situation** | Present the state of the situation that leads to the need to carry out the project |
| **State of the future situation** | Describe what the situation would look like after the project is put in place. |
| **Business objective** | State the goal based on your strategic plan |
| **Needs** | Do an analysis of your business + functional needs |
| **Suggested solutions** | • Description of the solution • Deadlines • Budgets / costs - efforts to deliver the project • Expected benefits - your return on monetary investment • Advantages and disadvantages • Risks |
| **Recommendation** | Explain why the project should be done |

Now that you have finished updating the case file, you must approve it. In the context of a company where several people are involved, a steering committee will put the proposed project in perspective with the company's strategy. The project will then be approved or rejected. If you do not have a committee, make an objective assessment of what you need to do.

Important Note: Not all projects may be feasible now, because they are not part of your business strategy. They can however be realized later. We speak in concrete project portfolio management.

**Identification phase (feasibility study or start-up):**

You have determined in the previous phase (pre-validation) that you have a good idea of project in the hands that fits with your company's strategy. Now, you have to determine its viability and economic implications in your business to prove that it is technically and financially viable. We call this step the feasibility study. This can, when done well, contribute to the success of a project. If not, it will contribute to its failure. In the corporate launch phase, the feasibility study will take on a larger dimension.

At this stage, you will therefore analyze the project to see if it is feasible. You will do this using a key document that contains the project memory: in project management, we call it Project Charter, while in business launch, we call it Business Plan.

Note:
You will find the example of a Project Charter attached. I propose here the outline of this charter. You will notice that it is a condensed version of the business plan.

| Section | Description |
| --- | --- |
| WHAT? | What are we talking about? What kind of project is it? What will be included and excluded? What is the product, service, problem, purpose, and end result? |
| WHY? | What are the reasons and challenges of the project? |
| WHO? | Who are the actors, the beneficiaries, the sponsors, the stakeholders, the managers? |
| WHEN? | What are the deadlines, durations, and planning? |
| WHERE? | In which places are the project, work, and development |
| HOW MUCH? | What are the numbers, statistics, reports, budget, and estimates |

| HOW? | What are we talking about? What kind of project is it? What will be included and excluded? What is the product, service, problem, purpose, and end result? |
|---|---|
| CONSEQUENCES | What consequences will the project have on the environment, the company or the organization, the actors, the stakeholders, the working time? temps de travail ? |
| MEANS | What asre the human, financial and material resources used? |
| RESULTS | What is the final objective of the project, the expected result and its indicators? |

\* If you do not have the answers to any of these questions, you will have to return to the starting box. You will have to research and ask questions because you cannot leave these questions unanswered

## Prototype

I also propose to you to prototype a project that will accompany your project charter/business plan. A prototype is a visual representation of what you want to do. It helps to better understand and present your project. If you want a new website for example, you will have to draw all the pages that you desire with the links between them. These drawings of your new website are your prototype. You will present it to key people who can give you their opinion and help you better define your need. As the saying goes: "a picture is worth a thousand words".

The prototype answers the following questions

| Questions | Description |
|---|---|
| *For who?* | *The audience we are going to touch from* |
| *Who wishes?* | *The target audience* |

| What does our product do? | The function of the product |
|---|---|
| Who is? | The utility of the solution; the expected benefit |
| Unlike? | What we are doing now, our competitors |
| Allows? | Key element that makes the difference |

With these two documents you can now go to the next step: detailed planning of what you will do.

**Definition phase (planning)**
Once the feasibility study has been completed and approved with positive conclusions, you will now have to provide all the information that defines the project. You will produce a project document called Project Plan. This plan will be subject to rigorous monitoring and control, using various methods and tools, to ensure proper project planning.

This planning phase will allow you to define:

- The organization of the project, i.e. the composition of the project team to be mobilized, the various experts to be solicited, the subcontracting to be called upon, the project manager or project manager to name, the mission letter to be drafted, and the management committee of the project to be set up;
- Scheduling is carried out with their order, duration, resource allocation, and technical resources as well as milestones;
- The potential technical environment to prepare;
- The project budget to be committed;
- The means to control the results.

The purpose of this phase is to design or specify what must be achieved or manufactured to achieve the objective. It consists of studying different solutions or technical and functional architectures according to the constraints of skills, equipment, deadlines well as fi and marketing aspects. The choices must then be validated by the creation of models or prototypes and possibly the marketing test (pilot). The differences measured will make it possible to rectify the choices that have been made (monitoring and control).

When planning a project, make sure you do the analysis and preparation: you must make the forecast, the budget, the scenarios, the probabilities, the alternative or fallback solutions (for be prepared in case of obstacles when executing the plan), and many other elements.

The project can be broken down into batches, into subprojects, or into building sites, to obtain subsets whose complexities are more easily controllable. The division of a project into manageable subsets is essential to the project's management, its successful completion and its success. The project division also makes planning easier.

If you want to build a website for example, you will have to:

- o Draw the website
- o Compose the texts
- o Correct and review the texts
- o Make the layout

Note:
Project management is usually done by a project manager, project manager, or a project manager. For effective control, entrust to a PCO.

**Planning tools**
As you know, a project is an idea that we want to achieve. As such, it is important to answer crucial questions that will guarantee its realization. There are several methods that will help you do that,

and here are two of them. I propose you two that will help you to realize your projects. Each has its advantages and disadvantages. They can be used depending on the type of project to be carried out.

## The what method

This method consists of answering specific questions:

What (actions)
- Who (the people involved)
- Where (the areas affected by the project, or even the places physical)
- When (programming in time)
- How (means, methods ...)
- How much (the budget)
- Why (reasons and objectives

These questions must be clearly answered to get the project off to a good start and ensure that project objectives are well defined and understood by stakeholders.

## The SMART method

When you define the goals of your project, you need to ensure that the latter is clear and precise.

"S": specific. You must be precise and clear. By entering "I wish it would increase my growth ... ", you are too vague.

"M": measurable. This is the encrypted data with parameters that can be measured. The example, "the sales department targets an 8% increase in the conversion rate in the Montreal area" is easier to measure than "I wish there were more employees collaborating on the corporate blog".

"A": Attainable. The defined measures must be achievable. For example, quadruple sales in one quarter is certainly an ambitious goal, but is it achievable? Do you have a well-trained team that can do it? Your attainable goal must offer you tools and you must have the support to accomplish it.

"R": Realistic. Be honest with yourself. If you like an idea, is it possible to implement it? Ex. Add an intranet connection to improve internal communications. Are you going to use it really? You must be realistic in your approach and anticipate change management or integration of change.

"T": Time. You must give yourself a date for achieving your goal to calculate the progress of the project. When you invest time and money, it makes sense to know if the project is going well and if our schedule is right. The project plan contains a set of documents that will be used to execute the project. Here are a few:

- The key document to be produced is called the execution plan of a project. This document will contain the different mechanisms of control and monitoring of the project, as well as the definition of what you want to accomplish. This document will maintain control throughout the project.
- The list of needs. This list will be in the form of specific requests to facilitate the task to the execution team.
- The project risk management document. This last document is an analysis of what could potentially malfunction during the execution of the project.
- Let's talk about risk. A risk is the analysis of what could happen with the project and have an impact on the goal defined in advance. This disruptive element can have an influence on the costs of the project, on the scope (what one wants to do), on time, and indirectly on quality. By performing some risk analyses, you have the tools to act when this disruptive element occurs.
- This contingency management must be done before the completion of a project. It is important to keep it up-to-date,

as it will serve you throughout the implementation of the project. It will help you greatly to reduce the unexpected and to have a better control over your success.
- How to do? Make a list of all the unexpected things you can think of and place them in an Excel file. Add a simple action plan for each of them so that you can act quickly if they occur. This document needs to be updated and monitored regularly as it will affect the success of your project.

| Description | Action Plan | When it can happen |
|---|---|---|
|  |  |  |
|  |  |  |

**Implementation phase (Execution)**
It's finally time to act! Here, you will try to start the implementation machine and manage the unforeseen events that may happen throughout the project. You will, therefore, execute what you have planned previously. The implementation phase is also called the operational phase of the project. It is supported by the monitoring and control of the project.

Communication is crucial to the success of a project, especially in the implementation phase. To ensure good communication between your team members, progress meetings will be held. These weekly meetings should be planned for the life of the project and should be part of your routine.

Content of these meetings:

- The progress of the project
- Challenges
- The next actions
- The budget
- Validation of priorities

The basic communication tools that will be used:

- The use of a pilot dashboard graphically presenting the progress of the project, thus helping the project manager to make the right decisions when planning changes. *
- A progress report that all project stakeholders will receive, containing the actions in progress and those that are completed

There are also daily work meetings that can put in place. These will help you get updates every day and be in perfect symbiosis with your action plan. By holding daily meetings, it will be easier for you to assemble all the information and have something ready. and functional before the ultimate end of the project. For an entrepreneur, this may mean getting revenue even before the project is launched.

**How to do?**
Step-by-step adds small parts of your project incrementally. This method certifies that everything added to the project brings an improvement without creating a malfunction. This helps to have better control over the delivery of the project and avoid failures by keeping the focus on the primary need of the project. As mentioned before, it is important to meet your team several times a week to establish the actions to be taken and to quickly resolve the difficulties encountered.

The meetings is 15 minutes long and answer three questions:

- What did you do between the two meetings?
- What will you do next?
- Did you have an obstacle that prevented you from moving forward?

Whether you are alone or in a group on your project, keep this a habit of taking small steps at a time.

## Monitoring and control phase

During this phase, you will produce the progress reports that will allow you to follow the realization of the project. According to the client's requests, you will present the data related to the budget, the schedule, the progress of the project, the management of human and material resources, what remains to be done, the milestones of what has been realized and next steps. You will do the validation by putting and comparing the metrics - the control bases you defined in the previous phase - with reality. The ultimate goal of monitoring and control is to remain proactive in researching project queries and taking corrective action quickly. Corrective action may require reviewing planning and implementation management plan to realign the project towards its non-constrained objectives and avoid the same problems. Monitoring and control are two inseparable steps directly related to the project.

For more details on this phase, I propose reading my first book: The Project Controller - PCO (demystify its role) by Nersa W. Dorismond.

## How to do?

The 15-minute daily meetings will help you validate where you are in the project versus where you should be, what has happened, and how to fix it to realign the project. There are several ways to perform a realignment:

- Reduce what you want to deliver (by reporting it)
- Cancel some elements of the project
- Add other elements to the project

You have to consider as much money spent, time, and results as problems.

Benefit: you stay in control of what you do no matter what happens.

*In summary: The establishment of a website. Above, I showed you two ways to deliver the project. The first is traditional, that you make a delivery from the beginning to the end. The second, which I recommend, is to make a delivery in stages; validate each of them before continuing and delivering the project. This incremental delivery method always delivers something usable and thus has better control of the overall project*

**Closing phase (Closing)**
A closing report will contain an evaluation report of the end of the project. In the final phase of the evaluation, a report will be produced in a way that will make the difference between the outcome of the project and its purpose. This will provide a point of comparison to avoid duplicating similar mistakes in the future. This is what we call lessons learned.

**The world of project portfolio management (multi-project).**
As an entrepreneur, it is rare to have a single project to deliver in our company. A multitude of projects are needed to bring the company's operations to a close. This is called project portfolio management.

We can define portfolio management, as a formal approach chosen by any organization to manage, plan, orchestrate and account for projects in order to derive maximum benefits. This approach studies, for each project, the risks, the real value, the funds available, the duration and the expected results. A group of decision makers, under the governance of a director, assesses the returns, benefits and priorities of each project to determine the best way to invest capital resources and the availability of human resources.

According to research firm, Gartner, the market for PPM (project portfolio management tool) grew by 11% in 2012. [1]

Here is a definition of PMI portfolio management: "A set of bundled projects and programs that reflect the short and long-term goals of a business while providing an overview of all projects. The components there are quantifiable, that is, they can be measured, ranked and prioritized. In general, their selection is based on criteria such as strategic alignment, the potential returns on invested capital (ROI), the size of the opportunities targeted and the competitive aspects."

In other words, in portfolio management, we take the time to align the delivery capacity of a project with the company's strategy by respecting the priorities throughout the realization. Let's repeat it: "Good project at the right time" "The right project at the right time". However, this notion is extremely complex since it involves a cross-business aspect and requires extremely tight control of portfolio data.

**Planning and top-down analysis, portfolio management**
In project management, there is a technique called top-down planning to help manage your project portfolio. This trend is characterized by company-wide decision-making. It concerns the portfolio of projects an organization must have, as well as the ability to make portfolio information more transparent through data mining technologies. We will talk here about choosing the right project at the right time so "Make the right project at the right time."

In addition, project management is also equipped with cost measurement tools, a set of control and monitoring tools that are found at all stages. Thus, each decision-maker can, at any time, know what a project costs and what financial resources are already committed. This specific characteristic of the organization in "project mode" then makes it possible to apply management policies related to "project management" (ex: forward planning, risk measurement, corrective action plan, etc.).

You, the entrepreneur, will have a multitude of projects that you want to achieve. To do this effectively, you will need to make sure to distinguish between the elements and take this dimension in your day-to-day business manager, and therefore project manager.

Portfolio management solves a series of difficulties often caused by poorly managed governance of a block of projects. It is not uncommon to notice in several companies that projects are left to their own devices, governed arbitrarily and without any specific direction line, such as a vessel without a captain.

The consequences can be catastrophic, for example:

- Launching projects randomly
- Too many projects running at the same time
- Mismanagement of human resources, which drag the project into length
- Bad project selections, some of which are unprofitable for the company
- Lack of governance when project dependency is not taken into consideration and the projection of expected benefits is indeterminate.

**How to do?**
The introduction of the portfolio management process in your company will make it possible to manage all the projects by considering the priority needs of your company, its capacity to deliver resources, and to counter the risks. The current manager(s) will consider all other criteria as directed by your company. By avoiding silo operation, optimal risk management will be possible

Sound portfolio management will present the company with a short and long-term objective chart while providing an overview of all projects. All components listed will be quantifiable, i.e. measured, ranked, and prioritized. Their selection will be determined according to a strategic alignment, the potential for returns on capital investments (ROI), the scope of the opportunities targeted and the obvious competitive aspects.

**In summary**
In the previous chapters, I summarized the essence of project management. The latter is a science of the deepest and most complex. There are several techniques, methods, and approaches that revolve around it, different schools of thought and how to do it. I did an overview of the essentials so that you, the entrepreneur, could start developing your business in project mode. You now have tools that will grow your business and reach your goals. Keep in mind that you can work in project mode regardless of your industry, right from the start

Throughout the previous pages, I have presented to you the most important elements to realize your projects. In the last part of the book, I will describe for you an example that you can use in your everyday life. You will also find attached the tools that I have described throughout the book.

"The foundation of theory is practice." – Mao Tse-tung

# Chapter 3: Annexe: A practical example

This example describes the steps of a project that most entrepreneurs will need to do: find financing. The example will give you an idea of the impact that project management can have on your business and will show you that you can get started in project management.

**Note:** There are also project management specialists who can help you with your projects, whether it's setting up your business plan or launching your product. Quickly equip yourself with method, people and IT tools to achieve project management. This will become second nature for you and you will avoid being among the 47% of entrepreneurs who have failed after 5 years. Management is not a guarantee of success, it is a guarantee of organization and control of what you want to do.

**You are ready to start your project**

The idea: It's your first business, you're optimistic, you quit your job with the equivalent of three months' salary in the bank and you're ready to start. You are confident that the amount you have in the bank will be more than enough to help you get through all the difficulties and propel your business to the top. No sooner has the business started than the problems begin: you have not adjusted your standard of living, you have made expenses for your launch that exceed your sales and now you have no money. It's a catastrophe !

The good news is that there are several methods to help you get started on the right foot. On the other hand, even the search for funding must be prepared and planned correctly.

**Goal**: Find financing for the realization of your business project. Finance research.

*My experience*: I am often asked by my students "How can I finance my business? ". My answer certainly surprises them: "How much do you need to start your project? Then follows a hesitation. To my astonishment, few people have a quick answer to provide me.

How can one build a house without an architectural plan, or do the foundations without a work plan? In entrepreneurship, the architectural plan becomes your business plan and the work plan, your action plan. I will go even further: the construction of the business model becomes the feasibility study of your company.

Here are the steps to follow:

1. Description of the need: manifestation of what you want to do
2. Establishment of a business case for the viability of the project
3. Starting the project at. Making the Business Case = Business Model (prototype)
4. Project planning at. Make a project plan i. Business plan ii. Delivery plan
5. Execution, monitoring, and control
6. Closure of the project

**Step 1: Description of the need: manifestation of what you want to do**

Let's go back to the first step where you have the idea to leave everything to devote yourself to your project and get started in business. Before leaving your job, you absolutely must make your budget or ask for help to do it. An accountant, an organization, or budgeting specialists will help you do it, understand it and give you ideas to maintain a realistic pace of life during this transition phase. In the end, you will have to make your own decision to continue.

Once your budget is set, you may need to cut your expenses in half. Add a risk factor of 20% to the cases where you leave at least

6 months of working capital in a bank account. Then write your project plan, fi plan and preliminary marketing plan. When all this is ready you can resign from your jobs. Warning! You will have to start making sales from the first day you quit. Some people manage to keep their jobs and build their business in parallel, the time to prepare the foundations of their business. They do it as long as possible. They leave their jobs only when they realize that they have a good idea, a good turnover and that the moment is propitious. It's not easy, but focusing on your business at this time will make it easier to make your budget a success, but it will give you a good foundation and help you get started. focus on something other than your living expenses during the crucial start-up period.

You defined in the previous step that you could start the project and that you were ready to go and get financing for your business. You must, at this time, prepare the Business Case also called Business Case.

**Business file**

| Sujet | Description |
|---|---|
| State of the current situation | I want to create my own company in website development to become independent and no longer work in a company. |
| State of the future situation | Have the necessary funds to launch the business |
| Business objective | Starting the business and launching sales. |

| | |
|---|---|
| Needs | Complete business plan, list of locations to submit the project |
| Suggested solutions | Business Launch Course - to make the business plan |
| Recommendation | Go get help to set up a complete project and ready, to be deposited and accepted |

## Step 2: Starting the project

Document 1-Business Model

I propose here to draft your idea of a business project. This technique is called business modeling.

**What is modeling?**

"Modeling is none other than organized thought for a practical purpose. The model is synonymous with theory, but with a practical connotation: a model: it is an action-oriented theory that it must serve. The model thus constitutes a possible representation of the system for a given point of view. It allows us to mentally simulate a behavior of the event. In other words, modeling is the possibility of putting a reality in the form of a visual model. It helps conceptualize a project or idea.

This modeling applies very well in the business world where the ideas must be structured to arrive at the success of a project. It describes, in the form of text and graphics, an ideal so that we can visualize the process and the architecture of our project.

This modeling will identify the variables that have the greatest impact on your company's bottom line. This will help you identify risk, better plan your operations and make better business decisions.

Modeling experts help predict the future of your business. Their crystal ball is a decision support tool that they develop for your company's needs. This tool will become your best business advisor! Business Modeling experts have advanced IT skills that enable them to automate your management tools to reduce the time required to complete repetitive tasks and avoid errors:

- Monthly gap analysis;
- Dashboard;
- KPIs;
- Monitoring report;
- Risk management.

**Make me a drawing**
Modeling is the possibility of modeling a reality. It is therefore the graphic representation of a mental image and its operation: when we have a model, we can mentally simulate the behavior of this event, our project.

Modeling is none other than organized thought for a practical purpose. The model is synonymous with theory, but with a practical connotation: a model is an action-oriented theory that it must serve.

In everyday life, everyone models constantly: we want to represent what surrounds us to anticipate his behavior.

In the business world, modeling applies to all levels and sizes of companies (small businesses, SMEs, very large companies) since we must model the elements of business and systems to enable the success of a business. project, a program or the implementation of a business solution

- To add a new application to a system, we must understand the business process.
- When we want to make acquisitions, we need to optimize our existing departments.
- If we have the dream of starting a business, then let's represent what we want to do.
- To understand the business process of the company, for the installation of a new software or a network, for the setting up of a website, to better understand the needs and better make the support and even for hiring new resources.

The advantage of this representation is the development, graphically, steps that lead to the realization of your project, while proposing the different paths to follow to get there.

Business modeling experts are committed to developing accurate, easy-to-use models that can evolve over time and are representative of the reality of your business. This modeling will identify the variables that have the greatest impact on your company's bottom line and allow you to identify risk, better plan your operations and make the best business decisions. This modeling is your reality, expressed in conceptual form, according to the defined needs. She enters the process of good project management.

**An example of modeling is the Business Model, Canvas**
The CANVAS Business Model is a powerful tool that allows a company to take stock of its business model. It represents, in the form of modeling, what you need to do to reach your economic potential. This model makes it possible to understand the structure and the economic path to put in place when you start a project.

Some people suggest that the Business Model Canvas as an alternative to the business plan. It is rather a complement and a must for the realization of a business project.

Condensed on one page, it will demonstrate at a glance what you need to understand, your sales process, and thus ensure you target the right clientele

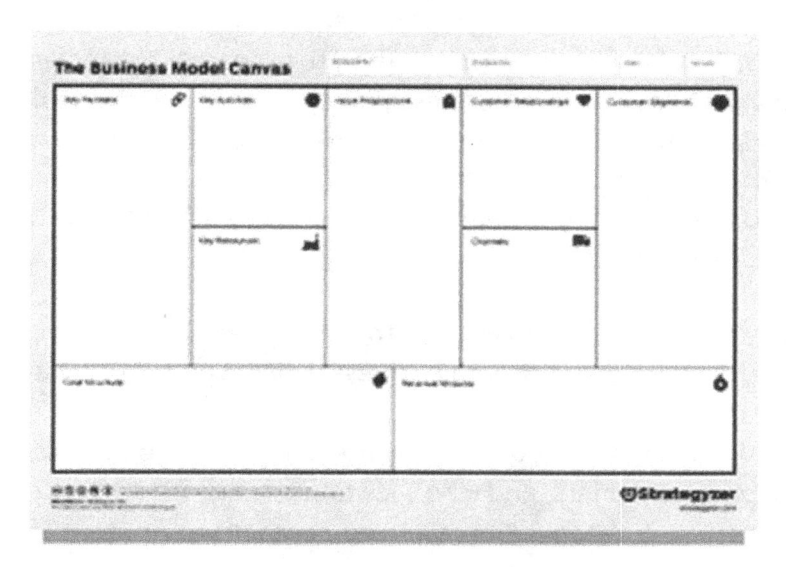

Now that you have thoroughly analyzed your business, you can move on to project voting planning

**Step 3: Project Planning**

Starting your business is the first project you will manage. This project will consist of launching the service or product you created. Afterwards, you will realize other projects that will spread throughout the life of your company. The following documents can be used for all the projects you have to cover.

**Document 1: Business Plan**

As part of the launch of your business project, you will write a business plan, a must for the success of your business. A business plan is a document that describes how the business will work: it is used to structure your idea. This summarizes and concretizes the vision of your company. It is considered an indispensable tool for obtaining financing and convincing potential partners. Throughout the life of your business, you will use it as a dashboard to guide you toward your goals and to ensure that you stay on track. When the time comes, your business plan will be used to prepare the transfer or sale of your business. The business plan is a very powerful tool that will help frame and structure the vision of your company.

There are different business plan formats and they almost always contain the following sections:

- Description of the project and the promoter: who are you, why do you want to start a business, what type of business will it be?
- Market Analysis: Study your clientele, how you go looking for your customers, and who they are.
- Marketing Strategy: How will you contact your potential customers to make a sale?
- Operational plan of Sales process of Human Resources
- Financial plans

The last section of the business plan is the financial plan. The latter provides the financial data necessary for the operations of your company and its start. Without money, it is difficult to go further. As we say, "money is the sinew of war," which means you need money to grow your business, or just to continue operations. It is therefore important to answer certain questions during the preparation of the plan fi

- What do you want to do?
- What products or services do you want to sell?
- What are your prices or sales prices?
- What are your expenses?
- What is your sales forecast?
- Do you have a marketing plan?

- Has your need been assessed by an accountant? If yes, has a forecast table of sales been made?

**Document 2: Extended Delivery Plan**

In the business plan, you have determined the amount you will need to get started. Now, you must know where the money will come from. To do this, you will develop a project plan or delivery plan for your project.

- Project schedule is to be realized
- The risk plan too

    Funding examples:

- Your savings, investments, or other types of investments personal
- "Love-Money": money invested by your loved ones because they believe in your project.
- Grants: * they are the best alternatives, because the money is donated by the governments and so, you cannot go into debt before you fully live your project.
- Crowdfunding: an innovative concept of financing research. It enables a project proponent to bring together a community of supporters who support it financially in exchange for counterparties, for a given period of time.
- Loan in an institution
- Self-financing: some entrepreneurs can self-finance your business start-up project. Here's how to go about it:

1. List the sources of income in your project (products or services)
2. Determine the cost to set up each of them
3. Choose the one that sells best and requires the least effort

4. Fund the overall project, step by step, using the revenue from the selected service or product

By applying this concept, you will be able to start and grow quickly.

**Step 5: Execution, monitoring, and control**

At this stage, you will put in place the research plan of funding. During this phase, you will have to follow and control. Advancing your funding search to make sure you collect what you need as money. You will also have to rework the plan if you cannot find the amount you need.

**For example:** You apply to an organization to borrow funds at a lower interest rate, but you learn that your request has been denied. So, you have two options:

If you had made a risk plan, you can carry out the mitigation plan written in it.

- You can review the initial plan and reduce the size of the project.
- Here are some methods to attract your customers:
- Make an email collection • Become a "youtuber"
- Create a blog • Sell promotional items
- Sell subscriptions to your services
- Make the sale of your products online

**Note:** It is very difficult to dissociate the execution phase of the monitoring and control in the life cycle of a project. This is related to the fact that controlling what you do will ensure the success and operationalization of your idea.

The execution phase is the most interesting, because you see growing and completing your project a reality.

## How will you monitor and control your project?

The monitoring and control plan is a crucial document for the success of your idea. Write when you will be checking your project, how you will do it and the expected result. By putting the odds on your side, you ensure your success.

| Follow-up step | Check the metric | Comment on the follow-up |
|---|---|---|
|  |  |  |
|  |  |  |
|  |  |  |
|  |  |  |
|  |  |  |

## Step 6: Closure - Celebrate and Prepare

You now have the money you need. We must celebrate! Be sure to note how it happened. This will serve you for the next funding search. Keep the course until the next funding stage

| List | Good point | Point of improvement |
|---|---|---|
|  |  |  |
|  |  |  |
|  |  |  |
|  |  |  |
|  |  |  |
|  |  |  |

# Conclusion

Project management is a rope of your entrepreneurial bow. This art which has been around for decades, and even centuries, will be the key to your success tool. It is essential to understand your role in this process. As a business leader, you are the cornerstone of the success of your project and the only one that can bring it to fruition.

Project management will be useful both in the start-up phase and the growth phase. It will be an asset to make sure that the current operations remain in a perspective of realization. You will need to realize projects to continue the growth of your business, optimize current operations, and get other contracts. Typical projects related to the development of your business may include the installation of accounting software, the opening of a new store, the restructuring of the human resources department, etc. By having a good knowledge of project management, it will be easier for you to undertake these development projects and ensure their smooth operation.

On the other hand, it must be remembered that this science is not a panacea, nor a magic wand: without a quality analysis and the establishment of effective control, it may lead to the opposite effect; i.e. to failure. You need to take the time to understand the techniques to succeed. Do not hesitate to seek the help of key people in the sector who can provide the necessary support for your success.

For more details on this phase, I propose reading my first book: The Project Controller - PCO (demystify its role) by Nersa W. Dorismond.

And if you need help, follow me on nersadorismond.com for more information

CPSIA information can be obtained
at www.ICGtesting.com
Printed in the USA
LVHW030810050121
675673LV00005B/1233